My Beautiful Cats

MARGARET COOPER

PAGE PUBLISHING
Conneaut Lake, PA

First originally published by Page Publishing 2024

ISBN 979-8-89315-282-1 (pbk)
ISBN 979-8-89315-302-6 (digital)

Printed in the United States of America

Elijah

Elijah

My Cat Elijah

I was born on January 10, 2018. My mother delivered four little boys on that special day. I was the first to see the real world, and I was as happy as I could be. Next, I was with three others, all of us ready to nurse and get our share. My mother was so happy looking at the four little ones, with all of us looking different. Of course, I was the best-looking having beautiful cashmere fur with a white stomach and paws to match it.

We found our way around a big house where my mother lived. It was not long before we learned to play, scamper, run around, and fight with each other, with me winning all the fights. Sometimes our mother had to take over and get us straight. She was a good mother, so full of love for each one of us and so pretty. Many cat toys showed up one day, and what excitement playing with so many mice and balls!

One day, my mother decided it was time to wean us from nursing. After all, she was growing tired, and we were all growing. New food came from the owners of this big house.

My brothers and I ate a lot of food and many times begged for more food. The new mother did not know what she really had with all four of us scratching, jumping on furniture, running, and chasing each other. I have long legs and could jump high over furniture and climb on top of many things so fast that it was hard to stop me.

All of us looked around and guessed what we discovered. There were four big boxes for us to do our popping and peeing in each day. Believe me, those boxes were used. The new mom had to clean them each day. What a mess it must be.

One day, all things came to an end. The new mom was growing old and could no longer take care of us. After all, it was hard sometimes with all four of us beginning to grow and explore everything. There were four big cat carriers in the room, and we quickly learned as each one of us was put in one and the doors locked. You can just imagine how frightened my brothers and I were. We tried to get out. Sorry, the door was locked. All we could do was cry. The car ride to another new home was long, and we wondered exactly what might happen next to us.

On March 1, 2019, we arrived at our new home. We saw lots of cats, dogs, and a few birds. What was going on with all the action? It was a shelter for all the homeless cats and dogs. The noise was loud, with dogs barking and cats crying. It was a short while before each one of us had a new place in a small space next to other cats with a feeding bowl, a water bowl, and a small litter box. What a change. My brothers and I were in the same space next to each other. I looked at them every day. There was playtime each day with other cats in a big room where running and jumping were great.

Most of the time, it was hard to get me back into the tiny cat home provided for me and my three brothers. I could climb so high that it was hard to reach me. I could hear people talking about this cat called Elijah. What can we do? I cannot reach him, and he is so determined. Finally, I would get down and be captured.

One day a visitor came and looked at my brothers, and I did not feel good about the visitor. I could hear talk about taking one of us home. I wondered why it was so soon. The very next day, one of my brothers left with the visitor. He was on his way to a new home. I was so sad, and my other two brothers felt the same way. What a loss for us. After all, we had all been together since birth. A few days later, I saw someone looking at all three of us. I had a strange feeling that another one of us would be leaving for a new place. In some ways, I was hoping it would be me. I was so beautiful, but I was not noticed like my other brothers. In a few days, my other two brothers left with someone for a new home. You can only imagine how sad I was that particular day. I cried so much and actually showed my temper when I had playtime. I felt so lonely and wondered why I was left. When would I be chosen to go to a new place? I was growing tired of living in such a small place and missed the old home with so much space to roam and play.

Another cat named Cuff lived next to me, and he was so pretty with heavy tabby fur. We played together whenever they put us in a big room to play. Someone was always looking at him, and I had feared that he would be taken.

One day, a visitor came and looked at all the cats. I could tell Cuff was one that was looked at more than once, and I just knew he would be taken. Finally, he was taken from his place and given to the visitor to check his personality and behavior. I knew Cuff had a temper. So I just wondered how he would behave. Sure enough, he was not, and he tried to bite the person. Cuff was put back in his home next to me. Then I saw two people looking at me. Oh, how I hoped someone would take me. Cuff had been rejected. Guess what. I was taken out to get acquainted with the people. You can just believe that I was on my very best behavior. They seemed very happy with me and talked about how beautiful I was. Of course, I knew that. I was now in the arms of someone waiting for a picture to leave my old place and go to another home. Papers were signed for me to leave and be adopted, with a chip put in me so I could be found if lost.

When I got in the car to leave, I was somewhat sad and began to wonder how much I would miss Cuff. He was my buddy. It seemed like such a long ride. After finally arriving, I was taken inside my new home. It was a big place for me. I got inside my new home. The first thing I looked for was a feeding bowl for food and water. I found it, and I then saw a big litter box for just me. I was a bit hungry, but it was too exciting for me to eat for at least a while. I just needed more time to see my new mom and dad, who had taken me instead of Cuff. I was the second choice, but that did not matter now. After roaming and being watched by them to see how I would behave and what type of cat I really was, active and wild tells who I am.

I decided to let everyone know what a jumping cat they had taken. I jumped on two high bookcases and did not want to get down after being called several times and hearing them say Elijah would fall and get hurt. I paid no attention and knew I would get down without falling. On those bookcases, I was now on top and looking down at everyone. Finally, it was time for me to jump down and get some food and water. It had been a different and unusual day for me. An afternoon nap was needed, but it was not for me. I needed more time to roam this new place. There were lots of rooms to explore and get used to in each room. I saw many things, but the big windows were what I liked best. I would be able to look out and see the outside. I was not allowed to go outside. They knew if I went outside, it would be hard to ever get me back. I saw two doors that opened to the outside. Believe me. I would look for times to get outside when the doors opened.

A nice cat house for me with a beautiful bed, scratching post, and many toys. Everything is just for me. Toys, mice, and a little white bunny who could sing when wound up. It was not alive. I heard them talking, saying this bunny belonged to a cat who had gone to cat heaven. The cat was Fluff, and I soon heard talk about him. He must have been special. I would get them to throw my balls up and see me jump so high. No one could believe how high I could jump. I loved to play with strings, chewing and eating the ends many times. I was soon eating edges off paper, and I would hear my name. Elijah did this, and he must stop doing this. One day I looked at the back of a door and saw a plastic covering on the door stopper. Boy, I took my claws, pulled them off, and left them beside the door stopper. What happened to this door? Look at this. Elijah could not do this. But they did not think I did it. The very next day, I looked at another door, removed the covering, and took it away on the floor beside a chair. Another mystery had not been solved. So, I decided to do it at another door. I was having so much fun doing this and hearing them talk about it. This time, I was not so lucky. I chewed on it and left it beside the door. The mystery was solved. Guess what. All the plastic covers were taken off the door stoppers. What a disappointment. I love chewing on plastic.

I was enjoying looking out the windows and the glass door, seeing geese, ducks, and birds, and wishing I could go outside. You know what I would do, and that is to chase them and maybe kill a bird. Geese and ducks were too big for me. It was such a beautiful day, and I heard a door being opened. You know what I decided to do. I hid behind the side of the door and quickly got outside when the door opened. I went off the porch quickly and began to walk quickly around the mulch areas on all sides of the house. I have such good ears and would hear my name being called. I paid no attention to these calls. I love eating grass, smelling flowers, and seeing lots of bushes. I soon heard someone sneaking around, and I knew they would see me. After moving so quickly and enjoying all of this excitement of being outside, I grew relaxed and decided to lie down beside a big bush. I then heard footprints and was all of a sudden taken back into the house. I knew trouble would come. This is what I heard. Elijah, you have been a bad cat and cannot do this for us. You know Elijah would try it again. Just give him another chance.

I am now being petted every day and loved so much being told how beautiful I am. With my good ears, I hear that I am such a beautiful, smart cat, and everyone is always asking where they got me. I could not be a lap cat with my long legs and body. They soon found out when I was put on a lap. I just did not fit the lap, and I was uncomfortable. I wanted to be loved, but I was not picked up.

It is now time for me to explore more things to do, like watching water drip in the sink, finding strings and paper to chew, as well as any wood I could chew on, but I was soon seen. The other bad things came from scratching on the rugs and a big leather sofa. Ma and Pa owners soon put a cover on the sofa. It had strings attached, and it was easy for me to find a way to play. Often, I would play hide-and-seek, find a place behind doors, and jump out to play. I loved to find a closet door open and hide there until I was found. Another thing I liked was rubber bands, and I found them mostly in drawers when I saw someone open a drawer. Believe me, I was fast, grabbing the rubber band, chewing it, and sometimes swallowing part of it. What a treat for me! The next thing I decided to do was jump on the doors and try to get the door handles to open. I soon learned that was not possible. I have a large basket for my toys, and I pull out the ones like best. Many times during the night, a toy is pulled out, and I run and play in the halls, crying for someone to play with me.

So many tall dolls are in rooms looking at me, but I am not interested in them. I know they are glad. I could do a lot of things I disliked with those beautiful dresses and hats they wore. I just stayed away from them and played with my toys. Toys with delicious catnip were my favorites. Catnip made me active and wild, running through the house and jumping on anything I could find. A real playtime for me.

Times for me to play are not always the best for Ma and Pa. So I choose to let them know by pawing at them from under a chair or just attacking them, not the halls, by jumping on them. This gets attention, and so many times I win. A ball is thrown in the room high above me, so I can jump and get it. This excites them, and I hear them say, "What a jumping, active cat who is also very smart and pretty." Of course, I know how beautiful I am, especially when I often look in one of the big mirrors and see myself. I bathe myself often so that I am always clean. I do think of my three brothers and hope they are as happy as I am.

When they go away for a day, I am not always sleeping. I would be told when they leave to be a good cat and sleep. That was not what I did. Jumping was what I did on bookcases, big clocks, cabinets, and refrigerators. When I would hear the car pulling in and the garage door being opened, I knew what I should do. I just went into the sunroom and got on the big chair, ready to greet them. I was always glad to hear them say I had been a good cat.

I was scared of a noise like the doorbell ringing. I would always hide under the bed until I knew what was going on and what was happening. Then I would gradually come out and get acquainted. Sometimes I was friendly, but not always. I was afraid of children who would try to catch me.

I was all by myself one day and heard the doorbell ring. I hid under the bed, as I always do when that doorbell rings. I heard two voices when the door opened. I knew it was trouble for me, and I must hide somewhere else. I could see two big men in the hall. I gradually sneaked out from under that bed and made my way to the top of the refrigerator. I got on top and fell behind it. It was a small place. I heard them leave, but I could not get out from behind the refrigerator. I tried so hard, but no way could I do it. It seemed like forever before they came home. I heard the car coming into the garage and finally heard the door open. I knew someone would be looking for me. It took longer than I thought before I heard someone call my name. I began to cry, but no one heard me. I could not cry very loudly since it was such a small place. I heard them talk, saying, "Where is Elijah? Did someone come while we were gone and take our cat?" Then they went outside to look. Perhaps they thought someone did come into the house for something and left the door open, and I went outside. A search was made for me. They came back inside and checked everywhere I might be hiding. I would hear my name called many times. I would cry, but no one heard. Finally, I hear them say, "He is in this house. I hear a cat cry, but where is Elijah?" Finally, they came into the kitchen and looked behind the refrigerator, and what did they find but Elijah! How happy they were. How happy I was when the big refrigerator was pushed out from the wall and I was picked up in someone's arms.

I am a bug killer. If I see a bug or fly, you can only guess how determined I am to kill it. I will not be satisfied until it is killed. Some bugs I actually eat. Other bugs or spiders are left on the floor and held with my paws until someone comes. My eyes are so good that I can spot one when no one else can even know a bug is flying around. I am known as the cat bug catcher.

One day, a big cat tree arrived with three beds stacked and a big scratching post just for me. I already had one, but not like this one. I smelled and explored it before taking possession of my new cat tree. I could kick more now, as well as scratch. Showing off was my big thing when people came to visit. I have long claws, and when I am showing off, you back away from me. I like to roll over and show my pretty stomach, long legs, and beautiful body. Rolling over makes me want someone to rub me and just say that I am so beautiful. I can never be a lap cat with such long legs, and I think everyone hoped I could be one.

I play rough and sometimes scratch and bite, especially when my nails need to be cut. I do not intend to hurt anyone, but many times I do, and see blood. Then I hear my name being called, saying, "Elijah is a bad cat."

I actually have two ways about me, and they now say Elijah has two sets of wings called angel wings and devil wings. I sometimes put on angel wings, be very nice, want to be loved and petted. Then again, I just put on the devil wings, not wanting anyone to touch me. I talk with my eyes and ears. Believe me, when those devil wings are on, my eyes get big and my ears stand up. With the angel wings on, I am ready to be loved, petted, and attended to.

When Ma and Pa went away for a little vacation, they decided to board me for a few days at the vet place, where I get shots. Being gone for several days was terrible for me. What a bad experience with a small place for me. I looked for other cats, but there were no cats boarding. Big dogs were there, barking a lot of the time. I did not like the food and refused to eat. I could not wait until it was time for me to leave. When I got home, the first thing I looked for was my food and water. I was so glad to be home.

I am scared of storms with thunder and lightning and stay close to my bed, hearing it rain and wishing it would soon stop. When it is very loud, I cry and go under the bed. Then I hear my name being called to come out, as the storm has gone.

I am growing and getting longer, but not fat. I have outgrown my first little bed and now the second beautiful red bed, which I wrap up in a little ball and go to sleep in. The talk of another bed has been talked about. Sure enough, they left one day, and when they returned, a big, new cozy bed arrived. At first, I had to smell, feel, and explore it to see if I wanted to sleep in the big bed. My other bed was left beside the new bed so I could decide. I finally decided to try it. I loved the new bed, which was much larger for me to stretch and sleep on. So now the old bed is gone. At night, Ma always comes in, tucking me in my bed and waiting right beside me until I fall asleep. I expect it at my bedtime and love it.

The housekeepers come every week, ringing the doorbell and coming into the house with brooms, mops, and vacuum cleaners. They all call my name and want to pet me. Sometimes I come to them, and other times I back away from them and go to my private place away from them, but I always stay near by guarding my territory and toys. They know I am watching them, and after they leave, I walk around, smelling everything. My toys are always there, and no one has fooled with toys in my basket. One day some children came and took my toys and scattered them all around while I was hiding from them under the bed. Children scare me. When these children left, I put every toy back in my big basket.

Riding in the big car is a thrilling time for me. I am in a big car taxi and can peep out the sides, looking at trees and grass on the ground when I am able to see it. I only go when it is time to go to the vet for annual visits to get my shots. I hate those shots, but I am a good boy. Of course, I hear that I am such a beautiful cat. I used to get my nails cut at the vet. I now let Ma and Pa hold me and trim my nails. I fight them holding me and seeing those clippers, but I finally hold still and let them cut one nail, two nails, and all the other nails. I hear them say, "What a good cat. Do you want some treats?" I get down and go to get those treats.

When someone visits, I sneak out and take a peek. I just get tired of being under the bed for so long. One day I came out, and no one saw me and thought I was still under the bed. I got behind the sofa and saw a long string to pull. It was just for me. I grabbed it and started chewing, looking up and seeing a pretty little girl having fun with her new game. I decided to be nice and play with her. She had pretty shoes on the floor. I love to smell shoes, so that is what I did. She loved to play with me, and I loved it also.

I talk with my eyes and ears. When I am scared, those eyes and ears show that I either see or hear something. If there is a bug or fly anywhere, I know it and go after it, not happy until I get it. Flies and bees are flying around, and I do have to be fast with my claws. I love doing it.

I am a spoiled cat who gets my way and is very demanding when I do not get it. That temper of mine acts, and I run down the halls, jumping behind doors and actually being a mean cat with devil wings. When it is time to get up in the mornings, I jump on their beds and let them know. Of course, I sometimes sleep with Ma. She lets me come into the bed when there is a storm or when I just cry in the middle of the night, wanting someone to play with me. When no one will play with me, I go to the basket of toys and pull out a mouse. I am a bad cat when my food bowl is empty, and that is not often. Believe me, I am fed well. My litter box is always cleaned each day. I am a clean cat, bathing myself many times each day. I love to jump on the bathroom counter and just look in that big mirror. What do I see but a pretty cat? You know something. I am a beautiful boy.

There are so many cabinets with doors I can open and just crawl inside. I love to do it by closing the doors of the cabinets and hearing my name called. "Where is Elijah?", is what I hear, but I still stay there for a little longer, letting them worry about me. Then I jump out and hear them say, "Don't do this again. We were worried about you." You know what? I will do it again. I love to see what is in those cabinets. I find some things like rubber bands and strings to chew on and books to chew the edges off. Other times are not like that, and I want to jump down.

What a day it was for me at the vet to get my shot and my annual exam, as they call it. I was put in my big cat carrier and put in the car for a ride. I cried most of the way and could hear them saying that we would soon be there. I hated being caged up and not having my freedom anymore; there was no way to escape. Finally, we did get there. I was taken inside and just put on the floor for a while. I looked around the room to see if I could see a dog or cat anywhere. There were none to be seen. I could remember being at this same place for a little vacation and hearing dogs barking and being afraid. I hid myself under the blanket in the cat carrier, hoping no one could see or get me. Then I was put in another room, waiting for my shot. It seemed like such a long time for me, so I stretched out with my long body and covered my whole body so it did not look like any cat was in that big carrier. I heard someone ask where I was, and no one knew. I was so quiet, hoping they would look more for me. Guess what. The doctor pulled the blanket, and out I came. I could hear the voices saying, "What a beautiful cat!" I was then put on the table and examined. Everything was fine, and I was ready for the shot. I was laid on my side, and the needle went in very quickly. No more shots for another time. I rode home and slept all the way home. When I arrived home, I looked and examined all my toys and bed. I always do this to see if anyone came while I was gone and took any of my things. Then it was nap time for me. What a day it was for Elijah.

Do most cats love music? Elijah loves music. When that big piano is lifted and someone begins to play music, I go to the piano and sit. Sometimes I get on top of the piano and look out the windows, and at the same time listen and relax. Of course, if I am sleepy, I fall asleep listening to the music.

One day the top was left open, and guess what I did, which created trouble for me. I went inside, and they began to walk on all the keys on the keyboard. I could hear them saying, "Elijah, you are a bad cat. Now get down right now." I decided to get down.

I love to be rubbed and hear someone say I love you. At night, I get in my bed and wait for a good night's kiss. My bed is so nice and big. I love it. I do sometimes get scared if I hear a noise, especially thunder. Then I go down the hall and start crying. I hear Ma telling me to come on in and get in her bed. I stay in that bed all night, but when it is time for me to get up in the morning, I let her know. I jump and play on the bed until she finally gets out of bed and goes to the kitchen, where I am given my food and water. Then I go to the big family room and ask for the window to be opened so I can breathe the fresh air and watch the ducks, birds, and geese come into the yard to be fed. They come close to the window, and I climb on the screen and wag my tail.

I am resting so well and trying to sleep. I just got picked up and am now waiting for my nails to be cut. I fight but finally yield, and the nails are cut quickly as I lay still. Then I hear them say what a good cat Elijah is for us. Most cats do not cooperate and have to go to the vet for their nails to be cut. I am just a good cat. After the nails are cut, I go to the scratching post and try them out to see if I can still do my bad things.

I am a jumping cat. I jump very high on the doors and try to reach the handles to open them. It is hard for me to take hold and open the doors like I do on the cabinet doors. Believe me, I can open the kitchen cabinets, close a door, and hide. I just like to see what I can find in those places. Many times, I knock things down and make a noise. Guess what I hear. "Is that Elijah in the cabinet again? He must come down." Then I jump out and run down the hall, giving them a wild chase. I like to climb on the desk and get under the desk lamp, where it is nice and warm. I get close and burn my nose quite often. I like to get on the puzzle table and pick up pieces of the puzzle, which are later found on the floor. Then I hear them say Elijah is a bad cat. When I am good, I hear them say, "This cat is a doll baby. What a good cat. Sometimes a devil and sometimes an angel." I hear this quite often. That is true.

Sometimes I just want to explore new things. Today I really got in trouble. I had been looking at the top of the shower doors in the bathroom and wondering if I could climb on top. Guess what. This morning I jumped so high and walked across, and I was afraid. After being yelled at and told to get down before I got hurt, I decided to jump, and down I came.

I am also looking at the top of the curtains on the windows to see if I can climb and walk on the tops. That would not be easy, but I will try it one day. If there is ever a bug, fly, or anything else I see, you can be sure I will not give up until I capture it.

I like to take morning naps where there is bright sunshine. I feel so good and do not want to be bothered by anyone. When I want attention and love, it shows by meowing and going where I can find someone to rub me and talk about what a handsome cat Elijah is and how lucky we are to have him.

I often hear about a cat heaven and learn about other cats who are now in that cat heaven. Maybe someday I will be going to such a place. Being such an active cat as I am, this is a long time away. I jump, play, and do bad things from time to time. Of course, I hear that I should stop whatever I am doing that is bad. I am a loving cat boy and will have a birthday in January 2024, making me six years old. I plan to live a long time, and the cat heaven can just wait for this beautiful cat, Elijah.

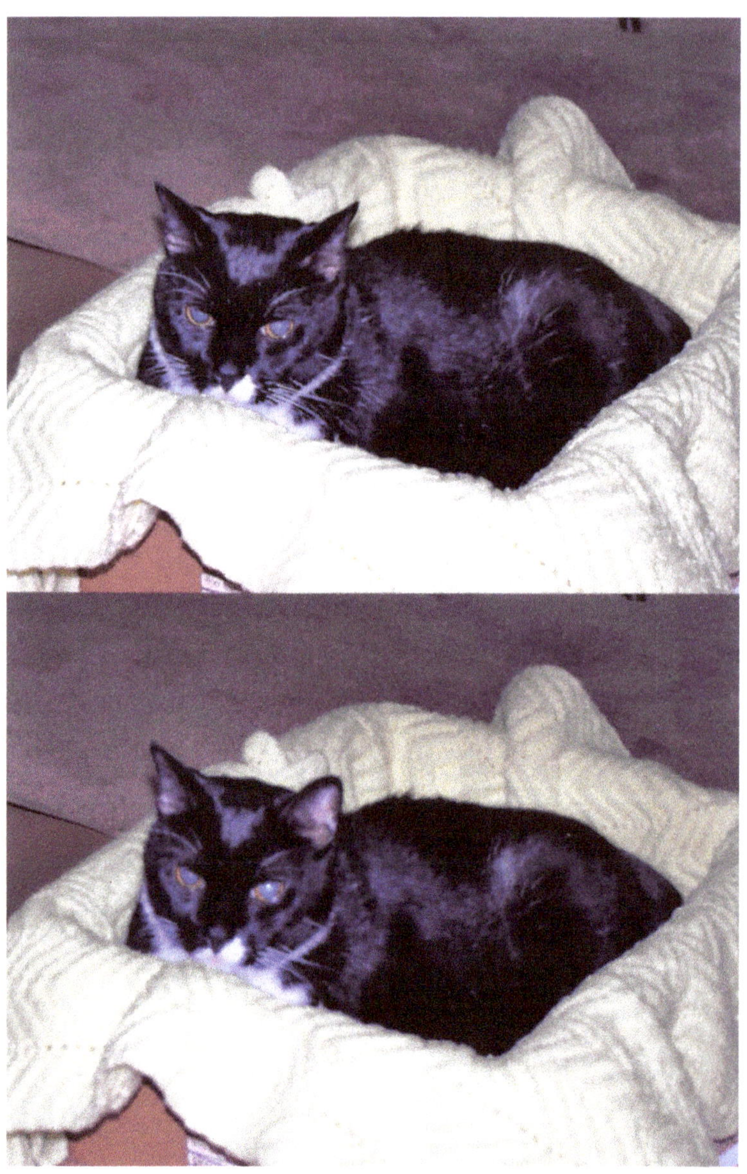

Jake

My Cat Jake

Jake was born on May 10, 1992, in a big barn with six other brothers, and at six months old, he was adopted by a college student who wanted a cat to love. He was such a beautiful tuxedo, with all the markings in black and white, almost like a pattern. She adored him and taught him many things. He lived here for a long time. After she married and had her baby, Jake was very jealous of the baby and wanted to be in the baby crib. Many times he was found in the crib, and after much thought, it was time to find a new home for the cat she loved so much. I received the phone call and responded, saying I would adopt him. I had just retired and decided it would be good to have a cat to love and train. So he arrived in a cat carrier with all his food and toys and a cat bed, which was really too small since he weighed twenty-one pounds. With him was the same litter box, which was also too small. So I knew I needed to shop for a new bed and a new litter box for him.

Jake and I bonded from the very beginning, and he loved his new home. He was a lap cat and loved to jump on my lap and take a nap. Sometimes it was hard to put him down when he had just taken a nap on my lap. He loved to eat. Jake was an indoor cat and could only go outside tied to a leash which he was used to and did not mind. He just loved going outside. Many neighbors would see him, stop, and make comments about this beautiful black cat.

Jake liked being tied to the front porch with his red lease. He liked watching people walk by. His greatest thrill was watching birds in the trees. Sometimes little birds would come on the sidewalk next to the porch. I can only imagine what he would do if he were loose. What a bird cat! He would be going after the birds. It was always nice to be outside, smelling fresh air. After his morning time outside, I would bring him into the house. Jake was ready for a morning nap.

Jake was a morning cat who liked to rise early, and he expected everyone else in the house to do the same thing. You would always know he was trying to get you to get out of bed. He would go into the bathroom next to the bedroom and start opening cabinet doors that he could reach. There was so much noise until you decided to cooperate and get out of bed. Many times, when you would not cooperate, he would get on the nightstand and try to turn on the lamp. Oftentimes, the lamp would fall on the floor, making a loud noise. He knew then there was trouble, and he would be punished. You find him in the kitchen, waiting to be fed.

One day I was busy with household chores, and I just looked out the window in the kitchen. Guess what I was. There was a black cat in the mulch area. I thought it was a dream. I could not see the whole body. I looked in the house to find Jake. He was not in the house. So I went in the yard, and there he was, hoping he could stay. Of course, he did not want to come to me. So I had a wild goose chase in the backyard. Finally, I brought him into the house, but I always wondered how he got out.

When Halloween came each year, it was time for me to give out candy. Jake would enjoy hearing the doorbell ring and watching the children on the porch wearing costumes and handing out their bags. He looked like a black Halloween cat. The children would make comments about him.

Jake was a people-friendly cat. He loved to have visitors and would make friends very easily, sometimes getting on their laps. He was a lap cat. After people left, he would smell everywhere they had been in the house.

Jake loved his food and water. Nothing was left in his bowl.

When it was time to eat, there he was, looking at you and asking for it. He liked to see water coming from the sinks. One night, the water was running in my bathtub, and he jumped up on the edge of the tub, grapping my hand with a nice little bite. I went to urgent care. It was several days before I would even notice or pet him. He was very sad that he was being ignored. He loved me so much and wondered what he had done. I finally let the guard rail down and let him get on my lap again. What a happy cat!

Jake hated to go for his shots, and he would hide when it was time to board him and take him to the vet. He was not well-behaved at the vet and bit the vet once. If he ever saw a suitcase anywhere, he grew sad and knew we were going away. When he got a chance, the climb in the suitcase was the joy he had, and it was hard to get him out of the suitcase so we could pack our clothes for a trip. Of course, he was smart enough to know what the next step would be. He would be put in the cat carrier and taken to the vet for a nice stay, which he hated. Since he was not well-behaved, I am sure they hated to see him come. He did like to ride in the car. Once he got there, other dogs and cats were worth looking at and wondering what they were like since he rarely saw cats and dogs. He enjoyed looking out the window and watching birds.

Raccoons were fed each night on a large deck. Jake liked to watch them eat out of their bowls. He would look out the glass door in the kitchen and just wish he could go outside with them. One of the raccoons had babies and would always bring them on the deck so they could learn to eat from the bowls. Jake would get excited when he saw the little babies.

Jake loved to go on the deck when we grilled. One afternoon, we tied him to the deck while we grilled, and he was having a good time. He decided to jump off the deck, and he fell below, hurting his back. The very next day, he knew something was wrong. He got in a basket in the pantry and did not want to leave the basket. He would struggle when he did leave and go to his feeding bowl. He also had a struggle using his litter box. We knew Jake had to go to the vet. So he was put in his cat carrier and taken to the vet. His back was broken, and surgery would be needed.

We decided to put him under, and believe me, it was a hard decision. We missed him so much, but it was the best decision we made on November 8, 2007.

My Cat Fluff

Having breakfast one morning after just returning from my aerobics class, I looked out my bay kitchen window overlooking my deck, and guess what I saw under the bench on the deck? A beautiful white tabby cat is half-starved and looking for food and a home. Since I had another cat, Jake, I had some cat food in the pantry. I quickly put some food in a bowl under the bench. Of course he was frightened, but he came back in a few minutes and ate all the food. I began to wonder why someone would leave a cat that beautiful, or perhaps wonder if he was lost when someone moved. I lived in Yorktown, which was a transit area with lots of military families. This cat appeared on my deck for a meal every morning. He would eat and leave, still looking around but very scared.

I decided to ask my neighbors if anyone had seen this cat or if a lost cat had been posted on a bulletin board at the clubhouse. Perhaps I had missed seeing it. One of my neighbors quickly responded. He told me this cat had visited his deck frequently. Since he owned three cats who were always fed on his deck, this cat would come and eat what was left in the bowls. The cat would fight with his cats. One cat named Pippin loved to fight with him. He had a three-legged cat that was loved by the homeless and never had a fight with it. This neighbor was feeding this lost cat.

After nine months, we still could not pet the cat. One night, after being fed, my husband was able to touch him while he was eating. You thought my husband had won a prize. He was so excited. Another neighbor called to tell me that he had seen this cat fighting with other cats in the neighborhood and what a tough cat he appeared to be. A large orange cat had now shown up on the deck looking for my cat, who was being fed twice a day. I always protected my cat from the fighting large orange cat. I decided it was time to name my cat. This name was a good fit with this cat's large layers of fur, so well patterned with colors white and yellow. The name was Fluff.

One day I received a call from my neighbor, who had the three cats, asking if we were still feeding Fluff. Over a year had passed. He had just had one of his cats taken to the vet. The injuries from fighting with my cat were bad. Of course, he had to pay a nice bill. He asked if we would share the bill for our shared cat if we had the cat fixed and shots given. We had fallen in love with this cat. It was a name for us to become new cat owners. We somehow got the cat in a cat carrier and went to see a vet. The cat was so dirty and shabby from being outside. The procedure went well, with all shots given and a nice bath making him clean.

Our cat, Jake, who was an indoor cat, did like to see Fluff on the deck eating a bowl of food twice a day. Jake would look out the glass door and paw at him. Sometimes, Fluff would put his paws at the door, giving Jake a warning to stop his fight and accept him. Since he was fixed, his personality has changed. He had become more friendly, but still very shy. Fluff stayed on the deck more, but he slept most of the time. We had several raccoons who would come on the deck at night to receive an evening meal. Fluff was not shy around any of them. He would stay on the deck and watch them eat dog food with water and cakes.

Fluff visited often in the neighborhood, making friends with one neighbor who had a German Shepherd. He still went to see the neighbor, who had three cats still fighting with Pippin. Fluff always seemed to win with cat fur on the neighbor's deck. Many neighbors would see Fluff from time to time and comment on what a beautiful cat we now owned. Fluff, of course, was still an outdoor cat. When we went away for a night, Fluff stayed outside, but Fluff was always there to greet us. He was very loyal and anxious to see us.

Fluff was a tough cat. He was seen by one neighbor fighting another rather large yellow cat. This yellow cat had been seen on many occasions on my deck, trying to pick a fight with Fluff. I would chase the cat off the deck.

One morning I looked out my dining room window, and what a shock! A little rabbit had been caught by Fluff. He ate the rabbit, leaving only a few scraps. He came back on the deck, acting as if he had won a prize. Fluff had become a friendlier cat, and it was now time to let him come into the sunroom to be fed each morning. Jake was very jealous, and he would search and smell the floor and often find some food left in Fluff's bowl. Jake would eat the food. He was a large tuxedo cat with a big appetite.

Since Fluff had begun to adjust so well, we decided that it was time to let him come into the kitchen for his morning meal and leave after he finished. Jake did not like it. Jake had been declawed, but he still liked to fight. Little did Jake know that Fluff still had claws, Fluff remained calm, avoiding a fight with Jake. Jake had a box of cat toys. Fluff had no toys, being an outside cat. Jake would never let Fluff have one of his toys. So we decided to get Fluff a toy. Although Fluff was only in the house for a short while, Jake would try to take Fluff's toys. Fluff was on the deck at night, waiting for the raccoons. He caught field mice at night. He always felt like he had won a prize. Bugs were always his favorites. He would wallow in the dirt and look for bugs.

Jake was only allowed outside with his lease. One night, we were grilling on the deck. Both cats were on the deck, with Jake being tied to his leash. Fluff and Jake started fighting. Jake fell between the rails on the deck and landed on the ground with a broken back. We took him to his vet. Jake was fourteen years old. We loved him so much. It was a tough decision. We had to put Fluff missed Jake and would look in the glass door thinking he may see him. He seemed to think that we were responsible for Jake being gone. He would come into the kitchen to be fed and look for Jake. He would go to Jake's litter box and smell. The litter was gone, but the box was in the usual place. There was a bench in the backyard where Fluff slept in the morning.

After retiring, we sold our home in Yorktown and moved to Amherst. The moving van came and took our furniture. Fluff was very confused and curious when things were being moved. He left and was gone for a few days. The closing of our house was scheduled for the same day when we said goodbye to our home in Yorktown. We went by to see if Fluff was there. Sure enough, there he was sleeping on his beach in the yard. We took him in our arms and managed to put him in the cat taxi, which was not an easy task. He knew things were not right. He loved riding in a car for visits to the vet, but he traveled two hundred miles to Amherst and cried and tried to get out of the car. All his freedom was gone.

After the bad trip with Fluff crying and fighting so hard to get out of the carrier, we arrived at our new home with Fluff. Fluff climbed on every window trying to leave us He now was in a large house with two floors. I must say he tried every way to get outside. Three days passed. We decided to let him go outside. He ran into the unoccupied lot next door to our home. I saw him disappear. Our lovely cat returned, and we were sad and regretful that we had let him go outside. Our neighbors had warned us about coyotes, foxes, and bobcats that had been sent at night. Around bedtime, we heard someone at the sunroom door. Guess what it was? Our beautiful cat had returned home. We were happy. This cat had a bad trip in the woods, and perhaps he had been chased by a wild animal. After a few days, he began to eat and settle down. He was now an indoor cat. Fluff still wanted to go outside. He was finding it hard to adjust to an indoor style of living.

Fluff loved to play with his cat toys. He loved to go around the dining room table with me, chasing a mouse on a string. He was still shy around strangers. When the doorbell rang, he would run, hide under the bed, and stay there until they left. Then he would venture to the kitchen, looking for food. Fluff would then smell everything. His favorite place was the glass-top table in the sunroom. How relaxed he was lying on the table and watching birds. The birds were not afraid of him. There were lots of windows in the sunroom. Often, a bird would fly and hit a window. Fluff would get aroused and ready to leave the table and let the bird know that he was in his territory.

Three months had passed. We decided to let Fluff go outside when I always went for a morning walk, returning in about an hour. He looked forward to this time, and he was always in the backyard when I returned. He was anxious to have his breakfast. There was one particular morning when he was not there when I returned. I called him, and finally, I heard his *mew*. He had gone to the vacant lot next to my house and ventured into the briars and bushes. There were grand hogs who lived on this lot. Finally, after looking for him, I spotted his beautiful yellow and white fur, and it appeared that he had chased a grand hog or perhaps followed his smell. After much couching and begging, he came back. The birds were not afraid of the cat. Fluff would stay on the patio table and watch them eat. However, if he saw crows, he would leave and want to come into the house. He loved to catch a field mouse and, on some occasions, bring one to the glass door of the sunroom, thinking he was bringing me a gift.

Fluff scratched on his post most of the time. One day, he was seen scratching on the leather sofa in the family room. Some other pieces of furniture had some marks also. After many pondering moments about what to do about the problem, we had nice furniture, and scratching was not what was allowed. It was our decision now to take him to the vet for declawing. When we brought him back home, he was very depressed. A special litter was required for three weeks. Fluff healed very quickly. I could not let him go outside for several weeks, and he hated not being able to go outside in the mornings when I took my morning walk. He knew the time and my exit door. He would be right at the door, trying to go outside with me. Being a regimented cat, he was at the door when I returned from my walk. He once again lost his freedom.

One morning, while Fluff was still outside, I saw Fluff trying to climb his big tree in the backyard. It was sad knowing he had been declawed and could no longer climb. However, he had turned his interest to chasing rabbits and squirrels. There were steps leading up to the sunroom. Many times, he would climb the steps to come inside after being outside. The rabbit catch had won. He came up the steps with a baby rabbit in his mouth and wanted to come in. We opened the door, and my husband tried his best to take the rabbit and save it. Fluff jumped off the landing and ran with the rabbit. We knew then that he was in charge. It took his hind feet to choke the tiny rabbit and place it on the ground. At least he did not eat it.

Fluff was now sleeping more and losing some weight. We took him to the vet, and he was found to have a thyroid problem and arthritis. A prescription was given for his thyroid disease. His litter box was in the basement with twenty-two steps. This was good exercise, but it did not help his arthritis. Fluff was never a lap cat. Being a Maine coon, this was his nature. He slept in his bed at night most nights. Sometimes he would get on our bed. He was sleeping a lot and not feeling well. He took his medicine, which was a struggle to get him to swallow the liquid medicine. He loved to eat cool whip and lick it off my fingers at night. This was his nighttime treat.

My husband developed neuropathy in his feet and could no longer take care of our large home. Several senior living facilities were visited and considered with the decision to go to the summit. We moved to a home overlooking a lake where there was a lot of wildlife, including Canadian geese and ducks in the lake. The house was all on one floor, which was good for Fluff.

Fluff was boarded at the vet on our move to our new home in Lynchburg. The day after our move, there was a heavy snow and ice storm. The roads were dangerous. So we left our cat at the vet for six days. How happy the cat was when he saw us! He was placed in his cat taxi and was on his way to a new place. He always loved to ride in the car. This time was different when he could see from the car window that there was a new direction, and he started to cry. Being such a smart cat, he knew something was not right. We got home and brought Fluff into the house, and he was so unhappy looking around, smelling all the furniture, and looking for his litter box, which he used right away. We fed him, but he did not eat. For three nights, he cried most of the night. I felt like there was a child in the house. He finally seemed to adjust, but he did like not having to climb stairs. At his new home, there were more windows to look out and see many geese and ducks strolling the neighborhood and flying over the lake. He was also seeing many birds coming to eat at the feeders every morning. The house being all on one floor helped his legs feel better. He missed going outside like he did in the mornings at his old place, and every time he heard a door open, he was at the door trying to go outside. One day, he got out when I went to the mailbox. What a job it was to capture him in the yard and bring him back into the house. He was now playing with some of his toys and wanted me to play with a mouse attached to a string. When I went around the table, he would grab the string and have some fun. By now, several of the neighbors knew he had a cat and came to see him. What a beautiful cat were the comments. Fluff began the walk more slowly and was not as playful. I took him in a little blanket and walked outside with him. It was a cold winter. He likes being wrapped up in his blanket. Two of my neighbors always invited us to come into the house.

Fluff was enjoying living in his new home and not having to climb stairs in his old home. He was happy to look out the many windows and watch the birds, geese, and ducks. However, it was sad to know he had thyroid disease. His medicine was increased, but it did not help. He began to lose weight and grow weaker in his walking. In three months, Fluff lost two pounds. Fluff was not a large cat, but the beautiful layers of fur made him look larger. We were told that his thyroid condition would only grow worse and perhaps damage his heart, which appears to be common. He started sleeping more and eating less. It was a struggle to give him medicine. When we went somewhere, like the grocery store, the cat was always there to greet us. Fluff would always let you know when it was bedtime for him when he would always have his cool whip treat licking some from my fingers.

One day, we noticed that Fluff was so weak and refused to eat or drink water. A vet was to see him the next day. He never made it to the vet. I woke up early and looked for him, finding him behind the sofa in the living room. He was lying very still and very weak. When the housekeeper left, he moved to the great room behind the sofa and stayed there all day, refusing us as we begged and tried to get him to respond.

I went to bed that night, wondering if he would make it. The next morning, looking behind the sofa, he had passed away. This cat was like another person in our home. We dearly loved him very much. *He* was buried in the pet cemetery. It was a sad day for us.

Margaret Cooper, a retired banker with a successful career of over forty-five years in banking, teaching, and managing many people, has published eight spiritual books. This book is for your enjoyment as you read about her three beautiful cats. Cat lovers will enjoy and love this book.